How to Understand and Win Your Spouse's Heart

Develop a deeper connection and create lasting happiness through mutual understanding.

Adegboye S. Aduragbemi

INTRODUCTION

Marriage is a profound journey of discovery, where two individuals embark on a shared path of growth, companionship, and mutual understanding. Yet, amidst the complexities of life, questions often arise about how to foster empathy, communicate effectively, and truly comprehend the thoughts and feelings of one's partner. "Understanding FAQ in Marriage" serves as a guiding compass for couples seeking clarity, empathy, and practical wisdom in cultivating a deep and enriching understanding within their relationship.

Within the pages of this book, you'll discover a comprehensive compilation of frequently asked questions, insightful answers, and expert advice tailored to the nuances of understanding in marriage. From navigating misunderstandings and resolving conflicts to celebrating differences and appreciating each other's perspectives, each question is met with empathy, experience, and actionable guidance to help couples foster a culture of mutual respect, compassion, and connection.

Through real-life scenarios, relatable anecdotes, and evidence-based strategies, "Understanding FAQ in Marriage" offers

4

couples a roadmap for deepening their emotional bond, strengthening their partnership, and creating a relationship grounded in empathy, compassion, and mutual understanding. Whether you're navigating the challenges of blending families, managing conflicting schedules, or simply seeking to deepen your connection with your partner, this book provides priceless understandings and applied tools to help you navigate the complexities of knowledge with grace, resilience, and love.

As you embark on this journey of exploration and discovery, may you find solace in the shared experiences of others, inspiration in the wisdom of experts, and the courage to embrace understanding as a foundational pillar of your marriage.

Let us embark together on a journey to explore the timeless questions, intricacies, and beauty of understanding in marriage.

Chapter One

Questions for communication

Understanding: The cornerstone of success in relationships

Emily and Daniel were two people whose lives connected in the quaint village of Willowbrook. Their love was built on empathy, communication, and a profound connection that went beyond words. Emily, a kind social worker with a huge heart, and Daniel, a considerate psychologist committed to helping others, met at a local charity function. They were drawn to each other's capacity for empathy and listening.

Their ambition to change the world brought them together, and meaningful conversations and epiphanies characterized their early meetings. Daniel was enthralled by Emily's generosity and her persistent dedication to assisting people in need, while Emily appreciated Daniel's sensitivity and his capacity to see the world through others' eyes.

Emily and Daniel found a strong bond and mutual respect as they spent more time together, which developed into a significant and long-lasting partnership. The understanding and acceptance they found in each other's embraces provided them with relief and comfort as they expressed their aspirations, dreams, and anxieties with one another.

Their bond grew stronger as they supported and guided one another through the difficulties of life. Emily and Daniel recognized the importance of understanding and embraced it as a means of forming a solid and enduring relationship.

As their love grew, Emily and Daniel committed themselves to one another by exchanging vows in front of loved ones in a touching ceremony. Knowing that empathy, compassion, and respect for one another were the cornerstones of their partnership, they accepted their positions as partners in understanding.

Years later, Emily and Daniel reflected on their adventure with delight and thankfulness. They were aware that empathy, communication, and understanding had formed the cornerstones of their relationship. Their relationship had only gotten closer over time, and they were confident that they could face any challenge together if they could embrace and understand one another's differences.

This brief story shows how understanding may serve as the cornerstone of a relationship. It emphasizes the value of acceptance, empathy, and communication in creating a solid and long-lasting alliance.

Never permit misunderstanding in your relationship.

Lily and Ethan used to be the definition of a match made in heaven in the small village of Willowbrook. They began a relationship full of love and understanding after meeting in college, where they bonded over similar interests and morals. But as they dealt with the difficulties of life, their relationship started to fall apart due to miscommunication and a lack of empathy.

Lily was a kind educator with a pure heart who valued understanding and sensitivity in her relationships. She constantly tried to put herself in Ethan's shoes and be there for him when he needed it. Ethan was a motivated software developer with a practical outlook, but he found it challenging to understand Lily's emotional demands and sometimes wrote her off as needless or unreasonable.

While Lily and Ethan's different ways of viewing things seemed like a minor annoyance at first, tensions grew as they dealt with life's ups and downs. While Ethan was frequently annoyed and overtaken by Lily's intense emotional state, Lily often felt rejected and unheard by Ethan's condescending demeanor. Their once-loving relationship turned into a never-ending spiral of anger, discontent, and frustration.

Their differences over their plans culminated in a full-fledged argument one fateful evening, bringing their understanding-related problems to a peak. Feeling misinterpreted and abandoned, Lily lost her cool and became enraged, accusing Ethan of not really knowing what she needed or how she felt. As a result of feeling overpowered and on the defensive, Ethan withdrew even more into himself and was unable to get past it.

Over time, Lily and Ethan's relationship continued to worsen, with their disagreements overshadowing any understanding or connection that may have existed between them. In a despairing offer to save their marriage, they attempted communication seminars, couples therapy, and even a trial separation, but it didn't work. Ultimately, they both lamented the loss of their previous understanding and made the painful decision to separate ways.

Years later, Lily and Ethan coincidentally crossed paths once more. They couldn't help but feel a twinge of regret for the understanding they had lost as they made small talk. They realized that their inability to understand one another's viewpoints had wrecked their relationship, and they wished they had placed a higher value on communication, empathy, and respect for one another early on.

This short story highlights the significance of empathy, communication, and mutual respect in building a successful and long-lasting partnership by showing how understanding-related problems like these may strain even the strongest of relationships.

Chapter Two

Basis of understanding in relationship

What does it mean to know your partner well?

Being able to sympathize with your spouse's thoughts, feelings, and experiences is a necessary part of understanding them. It entails paying attention, keeping an open mind, and making an effort to understand their feelings and ideas.

How can I better comprehend my partner?

It takes patience, sensitivity, and constant conversation to improve understanding in a married relationship. Try to actively listen to your partner without passing judgment, probe them to understand their thoughts and feelings, and show them support and empathy.

Why is communication crucial in a marriage?

In a marriage, comprehension is essential because it increases communication, develops emotional closeness, and deepens the bonds of trust between spouses. In addition to fostering a stronger sense of intimacy and respect for one another, it helps couples resolve disputes more skillfully.

What are some typical obstacles to communication in a marriage?

Lack of communication, presumptions or preconceptions, unsolved disputes, and disparities in communication or emotional expression are common obstacles to understanding in marriage.

How can we resolve disagreements and miscommunications in our marriage?

It takes open and honest communication, attentive listening, and a willingness to make concessions to resolve misunderstandings and disagreements. It's critical to deal with problems as they come up, try to comprehend one another's viewpoints, and collaborate to develop solutions that satisfy all parties.

How can we help our marriage grow in empathy and understanding?

Actively exercising empathy by placing yourself in your spouse's position, paying attention to their needs and feelings, and validating their experiences are all important aspects of fostering empathy and understanding. Having meaningful discussions on a regular basis and showing appreciation for one another's viewpoints can also help to improve learning.

What part does understanding in marriage play in forgiveness?

Since forgiveness enables partners to move past painful experiences and reestablish trust and connection, it is crucial for promoting understanding in marriages. Through extending forgiveness to one another for errors or miscommunications, partners can develop compassion, empathy, and a greater comprehension of one another's weaknesses.

How can we stop miscommunications from growing into more severe disputes?

Proactive communication, attentive listening, and a dedication to resolving conflicts at the outset are necessary to stop misunderstandings from getting worse. In order to avoid the escalation of miscommunications into more severe disputes, couples can create constructive communication practices like checking in frequently and allocating specific time for deep talks.

What are some tactics for enhancing comprehension when there is disagreement?

Active listening, recognizing and validating one another's emotions, avoiding placing blame or criticism, and looking for a middle ground or compromise are some techniques for enhancing understanding during arguments. If feelings become intense, it's also beneficial to take pauses and discuss the matter again when both parties are more composed.

How can our marriage change with time while still having an incredible feeling of understanding and connection?

Sustaining comprehension and rapport necessitates continuous endeavor and dedication. Regular communication is something that couples may prioritize, along with learning and growing as a unit and adjusting to each other's needs and relationship changes. Couples can develop a profound and long-lasting understanding that improves their relationship over time by putting empathy, respect, and admiration for one another first.

How can we get past personality or communication style gaps to improve our understanding of one another?

In order to overcome personality or communication style differences, people must have patience, respect one another, and be open to learning from one another. In order to reduce communication gaps, couples should take part in activities that highlight their individual preferences and strengths. They can also practice active listening.

What part does empathy play in promoting marital understanding?

In a marriage, empathy is essential because it enables partners to relate on an emotional level and validate one another's experiences. Couples can improve their understanding and fortify their relationship by placing themselves in their spouse's position and demonstrating empathy and support.

In a marriage, what does it mean to really understand your spouse?

Gaining a deeper understanding of your spouse's views, feelings, values, and experiences in a marriage requires more than just knowing them on a surface level. It entails active listening, empathy, and a sincere desire to establish an emotional connection. Comprehending your partner entails being aware of their wants and needs, honoring their uniqueness, and cultivating a feeling of togetherness and collaboration.

In our marriage, how can we foster a more incredible feeling of empathy and understanding for one another?

Open communication, vulnerability, and deliberate effort are necessary for the cultivation of understanding and empathy. Give your spouse your whole attention while avoiding passing judgment and making an effort to comprehend their feelings and points of view. Put yourself in their position and consider what they might be going through to demonstrate empathy. Establish a safe environment for vulnerability and connection by being upfront with each other about your ideas and feelings. As a partnership and as individuals, be open to growing and learning from one another, enjoying the process of gradually coming to understand one another better.

In marriage, how do we respond when we feel misinterpreted or ignored by our spouse?

Being patient, empathic, and communicating with assertion are necessary while managing feelings of misinterpretation. Use "I" sentences to convey your experience to your spouse without placing blame or casting accusations, and explain your feelings in a calm, collected manner. Be clear about the understanding and support you require from your partner. Even if you disagree with your partner, make an effort to affirm their sentiments by carefully listening to their point of view. Find areas of agreement and solutions that respect the needs and emotions of both partners by working together.

How can active listening help foster communication and understanding in a married relationship?

Fostering understanding and connection in a married relationship requires active listening. It entails focusing entirely on your partner's words and feelings while avoiding interruptions or passing judgment. To demonstrate that you comprehend and agree with your partner's viewpoint, summarize and paraphrase what they've said. It is a reflective listening technique. Pose open-ended inquiries to promote more research and comprehension. Active listening shows respect, empathy, and a sincere craving to create a profound connection with your partner.

In marriage, how can we reconcile personality qualities or communication methods that are different from one another?

It takes tolerance, understanding, and compromise to work over variations in communication preferences or personality types. Realize that each person expresses themselves and processes information differently depending on their background, culture, and personal experiences. To better suit your partner's tastes, be willing to modify your communication style and encourage them to do the same for you. Instead of getting hung up on minor points of contention, concentrate on discovering points of agreement and comprehending one another's true feelings and intentions. You may close the gap and cultivate a stronger sense of understanding and connection in your marriage with time and respect for one another.

In our marriage, how can we foster a greater comprehension of one another's needs, wants, and viewpoints?

Active listening, communication, and empathy are all necessary for developing understanding. Make time for meaningful interactions in which you can freely discuss your ideas, emotions, and life experiences. Put yourself in your partner's position and make an effort to comprehend their viewpoint without passing judgment to demonstrate empathy. Even if you don't always agree, pay attention to each other's nonverbal clues and emotions, and respect each other's sentiments. In your conversations, emphasize acceptance and respect for one another's backgrounds, beliefs, and goals. Act genuinely interested in learning about each other.

Chapter Three

Conflict Resolution Through Understanding

How can we work through differences in our personalities, communication preferences, and cultural upbringings to foster harmony and understanding in our marriage?

Respect, tolerance, and empathy are necessary for navigating differences. Understand that differences in personalities, communication methods, and cultural origins are expected and, when treated with an open mind and a spirit of curiosity, may strengthen your partnership. Spend some time getting to know one another's tastes, morals, and cultural customs. When needed, be flexible and make concessions. Be upfront and honest with your spouse about your needs and expectations, and keep an open line of communication. Prioritize establishing common ground and highlighting the unique attributes that each of you offers to the partnership.

In our marriage, how do we respond when we feel misunderstood or misread by our spouse?

Clear communication, empathy, and patience are necessary while handling misunderstandings. Be open-minded and eager to hear your spouse out as you approach the matter. Be explicit about what you need or want from each other, and speak honestly about your feelings and worries. If anything is obscure or confusing, get clarification before drawing assumptions or leaping to conclusions. Show compassion and understanding for one another's emotions, and cooperate to identify points of agreement and clear up any miscommunications that may have occurred.

How can we work through our cultural and ethnic disparities to strengthen our marriage via deeper understanding?

Managing cultural or ethnic disparities necessitates curiosity, openness, and a desire to share knowledge. Together, a couple can celebrate and learn about their cultural heritage, talk about their respective upbringings, and try to comprehend and value one another's viewpoints.

What are some telltale indications of miscommunication in a marriage?

Feelings of isolation or alienation, recurrent arguments that go unresolved, and frequent misunderstandings or misinterpretations are all indicators of a lack of understanding in a marriage. Couples may also observe a lack of emotional support or empathy from their spouse.

How can we, following a phase of disagreement or miscommunication, reestablish mutual understanding and trust in our marriage?

Honest communication, accountability, and a dedication to resolving underlying issues are necessary for restoring understanding and confidence. Couples can have introspective talks, express regret for any damage they may have caused, and collaborate to put methods for improved communication and conflict resolution into practice.

What are some tactics to help a married couple become more emotionally intimate and understanding?

Regular check-ins to talk about emotions and worries, participating in activities that promote connection, and expressing gratitude and affection for one another are all effective techniques for developing emotional intimacy. Couples should also make spending time together a priority and look for chances to have deep talks.

In a marriage, how can we strike a balance between our demands for autonomy and our need for mutual understanding and connection?

Open conversation and discussion are necessary to strike a balance between each person's demand for independence and their need for understanding. While keeping a solid base of knowledge and support in their relationship, couples can set limits and allow autonomy in areas of particular interest.

How can self-awareness help a married couple develop understanding?

Understanding within marriage requires self-awareness since it enables people to identify their feelings, triggers, and communication styles. Couples who practice self-awareness are better able to communicate their wants and preferences to one another and resolve problems with greater empathy and clarity.

In our marriage, how can we make sure that each partner feels equally understood and validated?

Both partners must actively participate and demonstrate empathy in order to ensure that the other feels understood and validated. In addition to validating one another's experiences and fostering an environment free from criticism or judgment, couples can engage in contemplative listening.

What are some methods or resources that can assist us in enhancing our marital understanding and communication?

Resources like relationship seminars, couples therapy, and self-help books on empathy and communication can offer insightful advice on how to strengthen marital understanding. In addition, couples can make use of online tools or applications that improve connection and communication, as well as ask for help from dependable friends or mentors.

How can we make sure that, instead of stagnating or growing stale in our marriage, our understanding of one another keeps expanding and deepening over time?

Curiosity, development, and continuous communication are necessary to guarantee understanding. Make time for frequent check-ins where you may communicate honestly and openly and maintain your curiosity about each other's thoughts, feelings, and experiences. Be open to your partner's criticism and eager to pick up new skills and insights from your exchanges. Make time for each other a priority so that you can strengthen your bonds and expand your mutual understanding. Accept change and adjust to new stages in your relationship, keeping in mind that comprehension is a process of learning that changes with experience and time.

How can we deal with circumstances when we have to adjust and communicate effectively because our perceptions of each other's needs or expectations have changed over time?

Managing changes in comprehension calls for constant communication, adaptability, and a readiness to change. Understand that when people grow and develop over time, it's normal for your wants and expectations to alter, too. Schedule regular check-ins so that you may talk to each other about your changing objectives, ambitions, and feelings. Discuss any changes you've noticed in your partner or yourself honestly and openly, and together, come up with solutions that meet your needs as well as theirs. Recognize that change is a normal part of life and relationships and approach the issue with empathy and understanding.

In order to avoid basing our understanding of one another on presumptions or prejudices, how can we make sure that it stays authentic?

A dedication to learning, curiosity, and an open mind are necessary to ensure accurate understanding. As you converse with one another, show genuine inquiry and interest in finding out about one another's feelings, ideas, and experiences. Refrain from assuming anything or drawing judgments too quickly because of prior thoughts or preconceptions. Make the effort to actively listen, ask questions, and, if necessary, seek clarification. In your conversations, emphasize mutual understanding and acceptance and treat each other with respect and empathy for one another's viewpoints.

How can we settle disputes in our marriage when it comes to each other's perceptions of personal space and boundaries?

Communication, respect, and compromise are necessary when managing differences in limits. Start by discussing your personal space preferences and boundaries in an honest and open discussion. Be open to hearing your spouse out and accepting the reasoning behind their boundary-setting. Recognize one other's requirements for privacy or personal space and respect each other's boundaries. To make sure that both people feel valued and at ease in the relationship, find common ground and make concessions where needed.

In our marriage, how can we foster a more profound comprehension of each other's communication preferences and love languages?

Active listening, observation, and empathy are all necessary for developing understanding. Spend some time observing and considering how your partner shows you that they are in love and how they communicate their wants, using both verbal and nonverbal clues. In case something is not clear or ambiguous, ask inquiries and get clarification. Put yourself in your partner's position and make an effort to understand things from their point of view to demonstrate empathy. To better suit your partner's demands, be willing to modify your communication style and be receptive to feedback. Make connection and mutual understanding a priority in your interactions, as you will find that a better understanding of one another fortifies your relationship and improves it overall.

In our marriage, how can we deal with circumstances where our past traumas or experiences affect our capacity to sympathize and comprehend one another's viewpoints? Resolving old traumas or experiences calls for compassion, endurance, and support. Acknowledge that your partner's perception and reaction to specific situations may be influenced by past experiences or traumas, and treat each other with compassion and understanding. Make an environment where people feel comfortable talking openly and honestly about their prior experiences and be prepared to listen to one another's worries and sentiments without passing judgment. As your spouse works through their past traumas, give them support and encouragement and place a high value on developing a sense of security and trust in the relationship. To address any remaining consequences of prior traumas and fortify your emotional bond, seek professional assistance if necessary.

How can we create an environment in our marriage where both partners feel appreciated and cherished for who they are?

Promoting empathy, dialogue, and a dedication to respect for one another are all necessary for fostering understanding and acceptance. As you converse with one another, show factual inquiry and interest in finding out about one another's feelings, ideas, and experiences. Seek to affirm each other's emotions and comprehend each other's points of view by practicing empathy and active listening. Be willing to accept and value each other's uniqueness and to be honest with each other about your own needs and boundaries. Establish a safe environment where both partners feel comfortable being true to themselves and place a high priority on developing trust and security in the partnership. Honor one another's differences and the unique attributes that each of you offers to the partnership.

Chapter Four

Understanding your children as a parent

How can I get my child to communicate with me honestly?

The first step in fostering open communication with your child is to provide a secure, accepting environment in which they feel free to express themselves. Urge them to express their ideas and emotions, listen intently without interjecting, and permit them to think as they do.

How can I strengthen my relationship with my child?

Spending quality time with your child, participating in activities they enjoy, and demonstrating interest in their interests and hobbies are all essential components of developing a close link with them.

Show your love and affection by touching someone, saying encouraging things aloud, and doing good deeds.

How can I properly punish my child without destroying our bond?

Setting firm and consistent boundaries, providing positive rewards, and emphasizing problem-solving techniques over punishment are all components of effective discipline. Teach your youngster empathy and understanding in addition to the repercussions of their conduct.

Which techniques can I use to resolve disputes with my child?

Keeping cool under pressure, paying attention to what your child has to say, and working toward amicable resolutions are some strategies for handling disagreements with your child. Prioritize establishing common ground through courteous conversation and stay away from power struggles.

How can I help my child with their mental and emotional health?

Fostering an environment that is caring and encouraging, promoting open communication, and teaching your child good coping skills for handling stress and emotions are all important aspects of supporting their emotional well-being. Keep an eye out for symptoms of distress and, if necessary, seek expert assistance.

What part does rewarding behavior play in raising children?

By praising and rewarding your child for desired behaviors, you can gradually reinforce those actions in them. This process is known as favorable reinforcement. Acknowledging your child's efforts and accomplishments helps them feel good about themselves and promotes their continued development.

How can I help my child develop autonomy and independence?

When you encourage your child to become independent, it progressively means letting them assume age-appropriate responsibility and make their own decisions. Provide direction and encouragement while they overcome obstacles and acknowledge their accomplishments along the way.

How do I deal with the difficulties of raising kids with varying temperaments or personality types?

Recognizing and valuing each child's distinct qualities and skills is essential to navigating the difficulties of raising children with diverse personality types. Adapt your parenting style to each child's unique requirements while encouraging acceptance and respect for their individuality.

How can I help my siblings get along well with each other?

Promoting empathy, cooperation, and conflict resolution abilities are all essential components of building a healthy sibling relationship. Siblings should be encouraged to cooperate on shared interests and projects, respect one another's limits, and communicate honestly.

How can I strike a balance between my welfare and self-care needs as a parent?

Making time for rest, relaxation, and enjoyable activities your top priority will help you strike a balance between the demands of parenting and self-care. Seek assistance from your spouse, your family, or your friends, and don't be afraid to ask for help when you need it. Never forget that taking care of yourself makes it possible for you to provide your child with the finest parenting possible.

Parents and their extended family

How can I put the needs of my immediate family first and still have a good relationship with my extended family?

Encouraging relationships with extended family members requires establishing boundaries and communication routes that are unambiguous. Acknowledge your priorities and constraints honestly and sincerely, and thank them for their support and engagement in your family's life.

How can members of my extended family help me in my job as a parent?

By offering helpful advice, emotional support, and life experience, extended family members can be a great source of support and direction for parents. Willingly discuss your requirements and desires with your extended family and encourage their involvement in ways that will strengthen your family unit.

How can I resolve disputes or arguments with my extended family members without jeopardizing our bond?

Finding common ground, demonstrating empathy, and using aggressive communication are all necessary while navigating disputes with extended family members. In addition to listening to their viewpoints and politely voicing your concerns, remember to set limits and put your immediate family's welfare first.

What are some tactics for involving members of the extended family in rituals and celebrations?

Open communication, adaptability, and compromise are vital components of strategies for involving extended family members in family festivities and customs. Talk about expectations and preferences with all the family members that will be participating, and be willing to modify traditions to suit the needs and schedules of all.

How can I set up appropriate limits with my relatives to safeguard the privacy and well-being of my immediate family? With extended family members, setting appropriate boundaries needs to be done with assertiveness, consistency, and clarity. Be ready to enforce your boundaries if required, and communicate them calmly and courteously. Never forget that upholding the integrity of your family depends on your ability to set limits.

What should I do if my spouse or kids and my extended family are at odds or tense?

Effectively managing problems or difficulties between your spouse or children and your extended family requires diplomacy, empathy, and open and honest communication. Promote communication and make an effort to comprehend one another's viewpoints, all the while putting your immediate family's health and harmony first.

Especially if we live far away, how can I help my extended family feel connected and like they belong?

Being proactive and communicating with extended family members is necessary to cultivate a sense of connectedness. Maintain regular communication via phone conversations, video chats, or written letters. Whenever feasible, try to attend family get-togethers and reunions. Express interest in your family's lives and successes and share updates on your own.

What part can grandparents play in the lives of their grandkids, and how can I help them develop a good relationship?

By offering their love, support, and wisdom, grandparents might have a substantial influence on the lives of their grandchildren. Promote frequent communication between grandparents and grandkids via online, phone, or in-person interactions. Encourage grandparents to impart their knowledge and experiences to their grandkids and cultivate an atmosphere of mutual respect and gratitude between the generations.

How can I treat my extended family members with respect and inclusivity when navigating cultural or generational differences?

Managing cultural or generational divides calls for mutual respect, sensitivity, and an openness to learning. Engage in discussions with an open mind and a curious attitude, trying to comprehend and value one another's viewpoints. Within your family, embrace differences and establish common ground by identifying similar experiences and ideals.

What should I do if the demands or engagement of my extended family in my life make me feel anxious or overwhelmed?

It's critical to emphasize self-care and create boundaries if you feel overburdened or worn out by the demands or engagement of your extended family in order to safeguard your welfare. Ask for help when you need it from your partner, friends, or a therapist. Be forceful in communicating your requirements. Recall that, in the long term, caring for yourself makes you a better family member and parent.

Chapter Five

Balancing Relationships and the Environment

How can my significant other and I manage our careers and relationships while keeping a healthy work-life balance?

It's important to prioritize self-care, set limits, and be honest with your partner about your needs and preferences if you want to maintain a healthy work-life balance. Plan frequent check-ins to talk about obligations, schedules, and how you might help each other achieve balance.

What are some tactics for handling disputes or conflicts that result from pressures or difficulties at work?

Active listening, empathy, and problem-solving are techniques for handling conflicts resulting from work-related stress. Establish a secure environment for candid dialogue, share your thoughts and feelings, and work together to recognize solutions that take into consideration the needs and priorities of both parties.

How can we strengthen our relationship while simultaneously encouraging each other's professional ambitions?

Encouragement, practical support, and active listening are all essential components in supporting one another's professional aspirations. Please talk about your own job goals and desires and come up with ideas for how to help each other accomplish them while still being in a close relationship.

What can we do to keep our relationship from suffering from work-related stress or burnout?

Prioritizing self-care, establishing boundaries, and using stress-reduction strategies are all necessary to stop work-related stress from negatively affecting your relationship. Establish a nurturing space at home where you can relax and rejuvenate as a family, and if you're feeling overburdened, get expert assistance or support.

How can we deal with issues that arise in dual-career households, such as juggling childcare and household duties?

Working in dual-career households has obstacles that call for cooperation, open communication, and adaptability. Based on each partner's strengths and preferences, divide up household duties. You can also look into opportunities for outsourcing work or asking for assistance from family or daycare providers.

What are some tactics for preserving intimacy and a strong sense of connection in the face of demanding work schedules and obligations?

Prioritizing quality time spent together, planning frequent date nights or outings, and finding little ways to express your love and gratitude for one another throughout the day are all strategies for preserving closeness and connection. Even in busy times, try to stay emotionally engaged and have open lines of communication.

How can we resolve disputes resulting from disparities in expectations or workplace culture?

In order to resolve problems pertaining to workplace culture, one must be empathetic, willing to compromise, and actively listen. Respect and acknowledge one another's viewpoints while cooperating to identify issues and common ground that uphold the values and beliefs of both parties.

What part can communication play in helping couples operate in a collaborative and encouraging environment?

Couples who work together benefit significantly from open communication because it fosters trust, transparency, and teamwork. To promote cooperation and friendship, solicit candid comments from one another and actively listen to their thoughts and worries.

How can our relationship be strengthened by acknowledging and celebrating one other's professional accomplishments and milestones?

Acknowledging accomplishments, expressing pride and respect, and providing support and encouragement are all part of celebrating one another's victories. Celebrate achievements as a pair, such as a project completed, a promotion, or a personal goal, and express gratitude for each other's diligence and hard work.

What should we do if one spouse believes that their career has eclipsed or undervalued the other?

It's critical to acknowledge and support one partner's feelings if they feel marginalized or overshadowed in their work. Examine strategies to help them grow professionally and increase their confidence, such as training, mentorship, or looking for new opportunities that fit their objectives and interests.

In our marriage, how can we help each other develop empathy and compassion for one another, particularly in the midst of conflict or disagreement?

Promoting empathy calls for perspective-taking, active listening, and sincere concern for your partner's emotions. Even if you don't always agree, show your spouse that you are paying attention to them and that you value their feelings by engaging in active listening. Consider the problem from their point of view and try to imagine how they could be feeling. Prioritize identifying solutions that satisfy your demands as well as theirs, and express sincere care and concern for their well-being. Remember that empathy is a valuable tool for fortifying your relationship and resolving problems with compassion, so exercise patience and understanding.

How can we handle circumstances in which outside concerns, such as financial hardships or work pressure, affect our capacity to sympathize and comprehend one another's viewpoints within our marriage?

Resilience, communication, and mutual support are essential for navigating outside stressors. Acknowledge that external pressures can momentarily impair your capacity for empathy and mutual understanding, and handle the circumstance with forbearance and kindness. Openly express your emotions and worries to your partner, and show openness to hearing their point of view without passing judgment. Recognize how external stressors affect you both and work to help one another during trying times to demonstrate empathy. Make self-care and stress reduction a priority if you want to be able to provide your best self to the partnership.

Despite the ups and downs of life, how can we make sure that we consistently and reliably comprehend each other's emotional needs?

Consistency in comprehension necessitates constant assurance, validation, and communication. Schedule regular check-ins so that you may talk to each other about your emotional needs and feelings. Recognize and respect each other's feelings and experiences, even if you don't always agree or fully comprehend each other. Assure one another of your love and dedication, and place a high value on developing a sense of security and trust in your union. Engage in empathy-building and active listening, and be prepared to modify your perceptions of one another's emotional needs in response to evolving situations. Make an effort to preserve a solid foundation of understanding and connection that can survive the ups and downs of life.

About the Author

ADEGBOYE S. ADURAGBEMI is a manager, business administrator, entrepreneur, and motivational speaker in Africa. ADEGBOYE has his BA from Yale University, IPMA from Adonai University, and a Masters in Business Administration (MBA) from the University of Salford, Manchester.

He was born in South Africa but is presently based in Nigeria as a motivational speaker and marriage counselor in institutions, sectors, and seminars with young and upcoming managers all over Africa.

Acknowledgments

I want to express my sincere gratitude to everyone who helped with the "FAQ on Communication in Marriage." Throughout this journey, their encouragement, insight, and support have been priceless.

I want to start by acknowledging the fact that, without God, this guide wouldn't have been possibly achieved.

And also to my spouse, who has always been motivating and supportive in making this task successful, I will always love and appreciate you.

I have many couples to appreciate who have shared their experiences, challenges, and victories with me over the years. Your openness, weakness, and tenacity have enhanced the book's pages and provided priceless insights into the difficulties of marriage communication. My sincere gratitude goes out to my family and friends for their continuous support and encouragement during this journey. Your wise advice, tolerance, and words of support have helped me get through the complicated process of writing and releasing this book.

I sincerely thank the specialists and experts who have so kindly offered their knowledge and skills in marriage and communication. Your advice and thoughts have improved this book's quality and depth, and I really appreciate your contributions.

Finally, I would like to express my profound gratitude to all of the readers of this work. As you journey through the process of communication in your marriage, I hope that the knowledge, direction, and encouragement provided within these pages will be a source of inspiration and empowerment for you. I sincerely appreciate your help.